COLORING BOOK

THIS BOOK BELONGS TO

LANKYBOX

COLORING BOOK

TEST COLORING PAGE

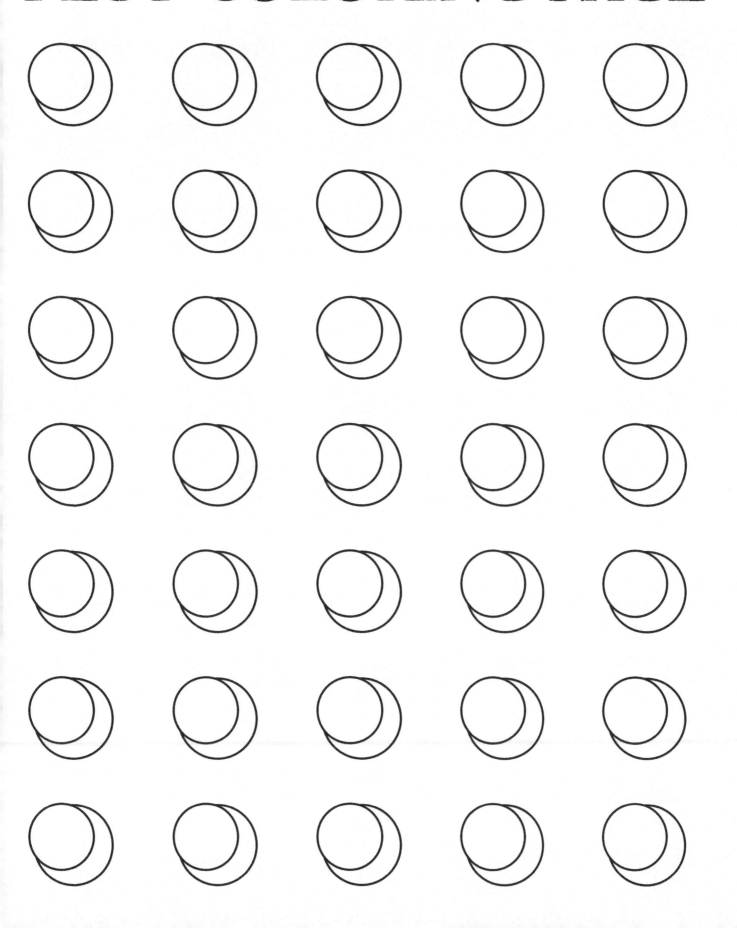

WRITE DOWN
WHAT YOU LIKE ABOUT THIS BOOK:

....

....

....

....

....

....

....

....

....

....

....

THANK YOU VERY MUCH FOR TRUSTING
AND CHOOSING OUR PRODUCT

WISH YOU ALL THE BEST
IN YOUR FUTURE

HOPE YOU WILL PUT YOUR TRUST
IN OUR NEXT PRODUCT

Made in the USA
Las Vegas, NV
02 December 2023

81962101R00037